ELECTRIC CARS

by Debbie Vilardi

D1361538

Cody Koala

An Imprint of Pop!

popbooksonline.com

abdopublishing.com

Published by Pop!, a division of ABDO, PO Box 398166, Minneapolis, Minnesota 55439. Copyright © 2019 by POP, LLC. International copyrights reserved in all countries. No part of this book may be reproduced in any form without written permission from the publisher. Pop!™ is a trademark and logo of POP, LLC.

Printed in the United States of America, North Mankato, Minnesota

042018
092018

THIS BOOK CONTAINS
RECYCLED MATERIALS

Distributed in paperback by North Star Editions, Inc.

Cover Photo: Chuck Burton/AP Images
Interior Photos: Chuck Burton/AP Images, 1; Shutterstock Images, 5 (top), 5 (bottom left), 5 (bottom right), 6, 9, 10, 13, 15, 17 (right), 19, 20; iStockphoto, 17 (left)

Editor: Charly Haley
Series Designer: Laura Mitchell

Library of Congress Control Number: 2017963432

Publisher's Cataloging-in-Publication Data

Names: Vilardi, Debbie, author.
Title: Electric cars / by Debbie Vilardi.
Description: Minneapolis, Minnesota : Pop!, 2019. | Series: 21st century inventions | Includes online resources and index.
Identifiers: ISBN 9781532160400 (lib.bdg.) | ISBN 9781635177916 (pbk) | ISBN 9781532161520 (ebook) |
Subjects: LCSH: Electric automobiles--Juvenile literature. | Technological innovations--Juvenile literature. | Inventions--History--Juvenile literature. | Technology--History--Juvenile literature.
Classification: DDC 609--dc23

Cody Koala

Pop open this book and you'll find QR codes like this one, loaded with information, so you can learn even more!

Scan this code* and others like it while you read, or visit the website below to make this book pop.

popbooksonline.com/electric-cars

*Scanning QR codes requires a web-enabled smart device with a QR code reader app and a camera.

Table of Contents

Chapter 1

The Electric Car

An electric car runs on batteries. The batteries store electricity. Electricity **powers** the car to move forward.

Watch a video here!

Most people do not use electric cars. Almost everyone uses a car that needs gas. But electric cars are becoming more popular.

The first electric cars were made in the 1800s.

Chapter 2

How It Works

Electric cars need to be plugged in to charge their batteries. They can be plugged in to a charging station or a wall outlet.

Learn more here!

Once the car's batteries are charged, the motor can start.

A controller sits between the batteries and motor. When the driver steps on the pedal, it tells the controller how much power to give the motor. This controls the speed of the car.

Chapter 3

Gas vs. Electric

Most cars today run on gas. But gas **pollutes** the air. Too much pollution can make air unhealthy to breathe.

Cars that use gas and electric motors are called **hybrid cars**.

Learn more here!

In the 1970s, a new law made car companies research cleaner **technologies**. This helped companies make new electric cars in the 1990s. Electric cars don't pollute the air as much as gas.

Gas vs. Electric

gas pump

People pump gas at gas stations.

charging station

People plug in electric cars at charging stations.

Chapter 4

The Future of Electric Cars

Electric cars can be expensive. They usually can't drive as far as cars that use gas.

**Complete an
activity here!**

But companies are working to make electric cars cheaper so that more people can use them. Better batteries and more charging stations will help electric cars drive farther.

Making Connections

Text-to-Self

Have you ever seen an electric car?

Text-to-Text

Have you read other books about new technologies? How are they similar to electric cars? How are they different?

Text-to-World

How would the world be different if everyone drove electric cars?

Glossary

hybrid cars – cars that use gas and electric motors.

pollute – to put harmful chemicals or garbage where they don't belong, like in air or water.

power – to give energy to something so that it works.

technology – objects created by using science.

Index

Online Resources

popbooksonline.com

Thanks for reading this Cody Koala book!

Scan this code* and others like it in this book, or visit the website below to make this book pop!

popbooksonline.com/electric-cars

*Scanning QR codes requires a web-enabled smart device with a QR code reader app and a camera.